Rolling Windows

Rolling Windows

Chris Campanioni

ROOF BOOKS
New York

ISBN: 979-8-9946050-0-4
Library of Congress Control Number: 2026932566

Cover photo by Nathan Dumlao
Author photo by Guy Aroch
Book design by Deborah Thomas

NEW YORK STATE OF OPPORTUNITY. | Council on the Arts This book is made possible, in part, by the New York State Council on the Arts with the support of the office of the Governor and the New York State Legislature.

50 YEARS
ROOF BOOKS
Roof Books are published by
Segue Foundation
300 Bowery FL 2
New York, NY 10012
seguefoundation.com

Roof Books are distributed by
Independent Publishers Group
IPGbook.com

Printed in Canada

C:\>

I am imbued with landscapes, it's the only retreat I can have.

Édouard Glissant

Treatise on the Whole-World

say the story
disappears
into its possibility

maybe she's born with it

the audience looks in thru the fourth wall:

but which you is I ?

we keep confusing the truth with a body
of evidence
forgetting the body
can only be recognized
after it endures
excavation

who said the west
moistens everything
with meaning

& at what point does a field
become a discipline & a discipline
become an organizing logic

my only provision
to have you
read this work
against the grounds
in which it was written

I for one
am not responsible
for what catches

my gaze, what is caught
there (somewhere between
the eyes & what evades

their orbit)
like medusa, his look
alone

hardened me
to a desirable
deformation

though I was always

observing
myself from
the inside

remember every image
has someone
in mind

so watch
my autobiography
as it sets

your stones
in mythic
circular patterns

ii.

Dream of a cameraperson entering the frame to install a second camera on top of the first; a second camera, *which has prior access to the discoveries of the first & is free to arrange them into bits of celluloid appropriate for every use.* Repeat: for every use, & for everyone to use.

iii.

what a time to be a light   a single beam of light
powered by deep
learning & maybe
she's born with it
maybe it's the making

of another
anatomically
imperfect person
from scratch

death of the content creator tho
my heart will go on

enriching the algorithm
without interruption

like melodramatic strands
of spaghetti code

in a stock photo
(late again for my thin audition)

I'm not a lyric poet & I'm not a confessional poet & I'm not
a narrative poet, so then what am I ,,, ?

♯ I'm the kind of girl u like (so cold so cold) ♯

notion of the skin
of your teeth
motion of the gag rule

how to perform a simple hip thrust
with accompanying audio
a longing for the lowlife

I'm letting it "all" hang out now
my unfamiliarity with american idioms

imported by
the smooth & uniform
trajectory of flight

passage from panorama
to detail
secrecy & decency

silicone or spit

subletting my transatlantic
consciousness for
an undetermined
advance

language (unless
printed) takes
up very little space

& more & more
readers
guilty of such common folly

assuming the stability
of the sign despite
the experience of
dispersal

what's the difference between a human brain & a hard drive
a hard drive & a tomb

how a word sounds vs. how a word looks
vs. what a word sees
          in the mirror

+ the accidental emphasis
of the tab key

our methodology:
clocklike transcription

seeking to transfer the common texture
of digital words & their printed kin

so scorn the horror
of multiplicity

agree to meet man
to man
seesawing btw

the socially respectable public
park &
the erotically active

underground
ejected from each

other's cluttered
timelines

in this fantasy
of a continuous now

chronological experience <
the spatial gymnastics
of recall

overcome by doubt &
submissiveness your saga

genesis 19

premonition to cast
the first
glance without

breaking or
taking
    leave of the flesh

    (look how the head
    glows before the spirit
spews forth)

my multiverse looms
in your rearview

barbarian

It's getting harder and harder to tell the colonized from the colonizers. Today one wore blue, the other white. Three days earlier the outfits were reversed. Who was it who was it who said revolutions repeat themselves, the same fantasies played out by different characters, on a revolving stage. It's true, too, on the television, where everything that happens happens twice or not at all. I have never used a blow-dryer. I have never used an alarm clock. I have never used protection. What is it within me that desires catastrophe, and did I, like all things, inherit this?

A student speaks of the one private jet every influencer entered, at the beginning of the pandemic, during shelter-in-place mandates and travel prohibitions, to craft the illusion of mobility. The jet has never left the ground. Sometimes I still imagine it there, permanently arrested on the runway, emptied of fuel, with neither a pilot nor a crew, without a destination, nowhere in which to arrive, but for this uninspired photo-op inside a lavish cabin, where faces that are not yours pose with a fake airline's sumptuous offerings. People give up their bodies for this. The beautiful game. I am watching with my legs laid out on the couch, as I prepare another seminar on overhearing, or even better, mishearing, unlcss I'm only there in memory, which is another kind of presence, another kind of death.

Sometimes, when I'm stuck, I'll rotate the page sideways and begin again, waiting for the moment the horizontal lines catch up with the vertical lines and how I can't soon distinguish between the two or can I. And if I run out of room, I'll flip the page over. And if I run out of room, I'll flip my hand over and use my palm. And if I run out of room, I'll use my uncanny capacity to forget.

I begin as I always do, by copying out the sounds that originate in the body. I arrived here in the same elevator you did, contorting my form beyond recognition as we each jostled what we came with to procure a single breath. I remember the stool I'd used to help mama wash the dishes. I remember running my hand along every shelf and dresser drawer, every countertop, as the lamp above my head gave off its unnatural glow, and I could see the extent of time collected on these most familiar objects through the dust circling in the air; the art of feeling useful. This promises to be a long list of short things. I know the age of the vertebrae is much older than the age of the mind and the heart. From sitting at lengths like this, hunched over so I can write more quickly than I can think—a rush I crave, since all this latent language, these delicious non-words, could drop at any moment—my lower back may be irrevocably fucked. If I require great abandon to do this task, I also require weekly Babylonian spa treatments. I think of my massages the way I consider the cadence and vibrations of the text. Beginnings are often tedious in their elaborate preparations, endings so contrived. How to achieve the intuition of a middle?

When I enter class, everyone is already seated, engaged in their stage whispering, audible from my seat in the audience but too muffled for me to make out words or phrases. What does it take to form a smile a real smile. She has never told me. Later, after the seminar on overheard things (misheard things), I'll pay my respects to the crescent moon on my short walk toward Fulton, passing all the scaffolding and shuttered offices, the *POST NO BILLS* signs that predestine renovation. By the time you read this, there'll be magnificent new storefronts; the crescent moon will be full; my vertebrae will require a brace; the studio made to appear as an aircraft will be a parking lot, which is what it was before its landlord started selling private jet visits for sixty-four US dollars an hour. Ralph H. had to wait 15-20 minutes after the occasion had already begun because they started repainting the set after the booking before us. Gaylord S. had to reframe their shots in post to avoid showing the damage to the set and furniture, which was dirty and visibly torn. Winnie L.

praised the extremely pleasant nature of the host and said the place was ideal for what we needed. Due to increasing demand, reservations for the studio in Boyle Heights, Los Angeles were soon being scheduled simultaneously, so influencers would not infrequently be caught in the background of their rivals' stories, unexpected cameos or an involuntary collaboration to each Go Live. My information keeps outdating.

One has the feeling of having lived through an old script. Destiny—where am I in all that? The national flag drapes around the human body as if a blanket, shrouding all but the jutting throat, the open lips, whose mouth is screaming, when I think to look, fellow travelers of other people's revolutions, other people's conquests of a home that is nevertheless not their own. More flags, each patterned according to a different schema, launched above each head like the mast of a ship. Ribbons of sun flaring onto the pitch as the day continues its march. Sooner or later, I think, as I turn my gaze from the screen, everyone switches sides, if not also uniforms, like every artifact of barbarism, like the barbarians that were so called because the Greeks couldn't figure out what sounds—what mumbling—were being uttered in their presence. Sometimes, when I'm stuck, I'll mute the volume and try to decipher your words from sight, remembering, after all, that anything that can be read can be misread and anything that can be misread can be passed along. A murmur in the sequence of unbending code. I would ask if pain changes you, but it isn't really a question, is it.

restored late renaissance oil

Start with a face. The rigid terrain of chin below a valley of cheek & underneath, the fan-shaped muscle that prevents a jaw from closing, assuming a jaw has remained (all this time) open.

Is the endpoint of every erotic impulse the thirst to annihilate? Genitals melting into the upholstery of this plush divan on account of the public prohibition of pubic hair, its illegality as consumer good. Together we accommodate the threshold between boundary region of the forbidden & the surreptitiously produced foreign export. Every image emptied of subject since meaning is rooted in desire & desire nourished by surface. The wind

shield splattered
with rain, each drop
dissolving
our faces like pixels
hatched
by a roving
lens
intentionally, I

Misplace my belongings in order to permit their latent recovery —to manufacture the joy associated with redemption, the relationship of losing to longing. No myth, remember, is singular.

His head on his lap, one of his hands stroking his hair. It's funny, if that's the right word for it, how many things one can think of & do in the span of two seconds. Head, lap, hands, hair.

Catalog, for instance, the most prized acquisitions of a life well-spent, all the time asking, sotto voce, did I keep them because they matter or do they matter because I've kept them?

chemical tang of torn receipt / credit card inserted or
withdrawn / dollars dispensing hypnotically / wrists
gyrating in repetitive motions / currency exchanged
in close crop / intermittent glimmer of ATM's greeting /
tempo of deep tissue reflexology / skin rubbed raw in
post

Because I want to inventory the things I've misplaced—objects & spaces & the people & feelings inside them—I draw us a map of their possible whereabouts. When does the improvised soundtrack I've made to accompany this geographic sketch jell into poem, into the dulcet gelatin of poetry? We grant our objects names but forget that they, too, have their own memories.

remember then this
pantry video play

list, remember
that we were

soothed, remember how
each of us counted

the beats before being
liquefied / together we

romanticize labor &
call it luxury, relaxing

into this massage
of repetition, anonymous

hands gripping numberless
goods in grid

formation   each loads
the other's domestic

hole as though home
were mega retail

outlet, overhearing
in spite of my wish

to be absorbed
another's face

& eyes & what the eyes
had seen   an iraqi orphan

who finds, scavenging
the waste of the world's

largest landfill
an american

sex doll
with which

to consummate
real intimacy

massacre of the past & the present
erotics of the inert & disfigured

mannequin intended for escape
(if escape means substitution

of the living
thing, if

rescue could mean oblivion
of one's self, the shame

of not having
a future) because we do not

know ourselves we take multiple
choice examinations & hope

to become the boxes
we've in turn replenished

& which guard us
from our tendency to fall (never

the less)
into feeling

♥

That was a movie, then, a colorful projection in a dark hall & the strangers I found myself between. Head, lap, hands, hair. Repeat it softly, without the mouth, without a voice, the body being extracted or implied. So you ask me to wear this G-string because you want to know if your fantasy of a flower blooming in the gardens outside Budapest's Hósök tere vibes with me, the way the thin ribbon passes between the curved flesh & firms against the small the very small of my back. I heard it was a good myth because of the hands, how the hands keep painting it. So stuck with thirst, instead of running my palm over the painting's photograph laden with scratches, dark streaks intervening in restored late Renaissance oil, I reached out. I held the nail for her.

intensities I was performing

before before before before before

this was a voice memo until it wasn't

meme-nto

(a style of accumulating images that belies the fact that every story is shown out of order)

it allowed me a space for intimacy, not with the other across the screen (whom I would never meet, never not ever. & this is exactly why), but an intimacy with myself

(its arcane origins, transformed into
physical form & rendered back to the virtual
via social media, are emblematic of
circulation's intensities)

I was performing myself, I said, being myself

it seems like
yesterday when we
sat on your bed

& you began to
guide me
to this current

tightness   how to
begin is
also where

So we selected that favorite scenario again from the options available to us under the assumption of infinity offered by the grid: its aspirations to display, its tendency to impose order. Under a false ceiling in the room reserved for banquet feasts, you smothered me with rose petals, as if you were

Elagabalus and I were one, just one, among any other unsuspecting guests to die before the mixing of wine with hot, very hot water.

on a different channel, bush
suggests americans go
shopping to prove
the terrorists wrong

And now the laying of different silvers and their specific applications inside the mouth; the sky, a spectral ashy gray against the smell of burning glue; my blond hair (not yet a dirty blond) in a pre-K photograph, the flat clarity of a superimposed backdrop, precursor to the logistics center of networked information, outsourced labor, abstracted bodies, resurfacing, in spite of its phantasmic processes or perhaps because of them, in the pantry's tessellated martyrdom, its devout absorption, the erotics of organized accumulation, our domestic reclamation of shopping mall aura. Best explained by Benjamin's suspicions of system and his compulsion, nevertheless, for optimizing erstwhile Parisian arcades into ornamental convolutes. How I ritually return my newly acquired items to my own interior's superstructure of holes and surfaces after cathartically unboxing each piece of merchandise. The fires, too, have returned. We hide from ourselves (our own fears our own desires) in an IKEA near the shipping yard; count the moments between the elevation of a silent object and its bombastic scan. The telltale hum of black holes merging in the early universe.

unexpectedly human

Behind or underneath every concept of an internet is a cooling system that runs on water & water that is coming

to a close, as in cleaned
out, wasted & exhausted, people also
ask why do data
centers continuously use more
water instead of recycling the water
that's been heated, pumped & poured
over the big fibre boards while the fan
blows outside
air past them? whether what's heated
is ever truly returned, whether I am also
ever inside the body as I kick
my legs off
the ground in incremental
variations is another question
consider synaptic
gaps in visual stimuli, panorama of moving
buildings in the distance that is morning
light breaking
against solid beams
of steel like two nerves
gliding across each other above
the contaminated river still
glistening when I smile
under my mask, the skin's
brief reprieve or redemption
of the eyes: a channel
of freighted passage, trashed plastics, &
my biodegradable
lungs contracting on account
of the air being overall a poor
conductor of electricity
nevertheless I detect liquid
in the lightning
cable, recall preservation's

adjacency to ownership &
possession plus
the precondition of loss or absence
that begets longing
as an operator in nepal
asks if I would like my organs
autoshipped   in some nations
I am an asset in others
a spy & if not a spy
then a surveilled object
please repeat
after me: extract the footage
between receiving raw materials
& shipping finished
goods in the supply
chain command
center then overlay
an audio track used
for calisthenics. all that exists
will scan & crystal
as code, all that is named
can be sorted
I've never seen
two people happier
to be in the blast radius
of airborne particulate detonation. yet
to photograph this scene
is to violate the sensations
occasioned by being
& behind this window
another window. so static
each slat of flesh; film
paused
at what feels
like an appropriate
juncture to flex
another vessel

we are carried or contained
by. The window advertisement for TD Bank's online banking system shows a man in suit and tie, legs bent, one foot held by gravity, one arm flung skyward, holding his cell as if it were a glow stick. *Bank like nobody's watching.* And in larger type, the phrase *Unexpectedly Human.*

I so often want to say out loud: what is it I am right now missing? And have these things, outmoded or augmented, really evaporated from our lives? Or is it desire itself that has disappeared?—pixelated and outsourced to an automated server, which nevertheless promises humanity's reemergence in each transaction.

Scanning my phone so much and all the time to purchase things or simply to pass has the tendency to make me forget it is my money that I am spending. Corporate benediction: to make consumers forget we are consuming even and especially during the calm moment of consumption, the moment of our withdrawal.

What is the name of the sensation people feel after watching another person restock their pantry across a screen. How long does undeveloped film last. In which direction do pacifiers go. What to say when someone dies.

I reshuffle my recent search history and consider banking like nobody's watching, forgetting for a moment where I am and how arduous the transition to the Anthropocene. Consider, instead: the swift slip of see-through doors admitting access to telephone booths, and an operator's voice, anonymous, intimate, asking about my wish for a collect call, and busy signals, and dial-up modems, and dial tones more generally. Hanging up on somebody, anybody. The thrill of it, the feeling of empowerment, abandonment, at least until the next call, an apology made or retracted, the rehearsal of commitment, a bid for forgiveness, devotion, disintegration, the dreamache of being picked up, discarded, et cetera. Later today a student will ask what that must have felt like, having never felt it themselves. I heard the experience of exile is akin to the custodian who traverses disparate spaces, collecting sounds. But what happens when the sounds, too, have already vanished? Because of the intensive compression that occurs when content produced for a traditional cinema is streamed through an app on a television, mobile phone, or tablet, many viewers express an inability to identify what sounds they are hearing, or mishearing. Some will adjust their volume settings; others opt for subtitles. Though there are those of us who, like me, no longer want to know who speaks or what is being said, what is spoken through the mouth or overheard by the eye. When I look at old photographs—the paper kind, inserted between folds of translucent plastic in an album—I try to insert a voice on top of each face, as if I were a sound engineer or a video dubber. I heard that William S. Burroughs once said if I had a talking picture of you, would I still need you? I heard the best the very best part of the pizza is the bottom. If you're holding, as we exchange age, sex, and location, the slice with one hand to cup the folds of heaving crust. But my poll remains inconclusive and unreliable. A problem or limit intrinsic to the medium. What do we remember of a person except for the grain of their voice? A voice that does not quite come off with the device I've used to record this, in the hopes of returning the body behind, the body obscured by the recording.

What does the album remember, as a picture is returned to its place or repositioned in another sequence? I can't help but lay my palm against this paper copy and produce a click, because my favorite photographs are the ones I've imaged again. See how my own hand veers into legibility, the curve of my beheaded neck trespassing inside the border of the frame, where a lit-up marquee signals filling station; a part of me gets grafted onto someone else's memory post facto, unless it's the reverse, that the memory comes before the experience. And experience, under pretext of immediacy, arrives secondhand. What are we here for I often wonder but to get into another's time and space, to conjure the improbable moment of relation?

The passenger to my left, if you're looking at me as you read this, has been asked to translate the phrase "my son needs a small suitcase" into Spanish. Balloons burst in the backdrop if he succeeds, and a green owl will dance. I get off at the next stop to imagine an alternative trajectory. Maybe what the son needs is potable water.

rolling windows

rhythm glimpses in passing
as it ripples across a bodice
or bodiless corset
archaic, alteration
of bodies—alliteration

of an exit sign
in french or the sign
itself, the rhythm
again: a desire
as movement, or feedback

loop in which
I continually shrink
into the other across
the screen I wanna
know your search history

I wanna feel
your message when
I receive it when you are
received by me
now my neighbor

playing her face
live as I type this we're
expecting a smooth
ride over the atlantic &
pleasant weather

v.1.1
forced confessions:

sometimes all I want is cheek kisses
sometimes I want kisses between the cheeks

v.2.o
did you feel the story coming
did you feel yourself
escaping death into
the haven
of our internet
(my only child
who is me)

v.1.2
music & film   past & present   analog & digital
merge here in an ~~immersive~~ emergent body

if I had a window to roll down I'd roll down my window for
you but no one

makes rolling
windows anymore

v.3.o
delayed in the moment before
we meet at the boulangerie
in a game with your
carefully maintained assortment
of brioche with which
we will siphon
a rolodex of taste sensations need
-lessly <<word missing>> our public
masquerade the best
non-fuck of my life
the best tracking device held under
my thumb the best
way to plant
a bug on someone you
place your piece on a part

of the body that one
would never look at even
in the private gaze
of the mirror (at this point

v.4.o

The artist says he became aware of his connection to the universe on June 16, 1965, at dawn, when you saw my shadow dragging across the side of Stromboli

v.5.o

I really admire your body of work I mean I really admire the work coming out of your body I mean I really admire how your body works I mean I really admire both work & bodies working both the body & the body of work the work & what's outside the work the words & the mouth that feels the words the lips that taste the words the ears that hear the words the digits that write them in the work or on the body

v.3.1

you are asked if you'd rather
stroll languidly past the royal gardens or
ascend the winding via valeria to reach
the duomo di taormina, now used as an exposed
brick entrance   a stage set
called giancarlo de carlo's
trattoria)

v.6.o

The morning I return to Catania, by boat, the Diciotti also disembarks, meters away, with nine hundred and thirty-seven passengers on board, & two corpses

v.4.1

some strange
voices aren't
clear before
my unlikely
conversion
kind of
me
the same
who needs that
control
who needs that
to understand
why I remember all
the lines
I should say
your face
counts
the beats
as in a treatment
our thin film
feeling
me up
again

v.7.0

These one hundred & fifty latex masks are self-portraits of the artist, all of them the same, which creates a contiguity between self-effacement & self-promotion

v.8.0

As we ride to the airport (you & I) from the back of the Alibus I see my last snapshot of Mount Etna, edging a silhouette across the clouds it melts against, & farther underneath, as we turn the corner (you & I), a message hastily graffiti'd against the edifice of a brick building that anyone could see or would see or will see or sees from any distance upon arriving at port

v.9.o
he asked how I liked it & I said well
it stays in your mouth

v.5.1
To marvel or wonder (at), to feel or show admiration (for), to respect or regard with astonishment & wonder

that parasitic urge
to supplicate
a host

Perhaps I will return (to this later)

v.7.1
I like to think of this project in at least three ways

v.8.1

*REFUGEES ARE
WELCOME*

v.10.o
the levi's sky & my
own flesh slicked
with the smell
of audiovisual

<<word missing>> just before
sunset & a pendulate
fan we turned
on to keep

us from stopping so much
of this can be imitated
just by watching
the film's opening

{eleven minutes}

v.11.o

Every student on every park bench in the Giardino Bellini is reading Walter Benjamin's letters to Theodor Adorno & at the same time painting my portrait or several hundred portraits of a face that resembles mine & no other in the light of Catania in the middle of day in the genderless June sun of my curated memories I got sent to the principal for being rude I got sent to the principal for being nude really I lack the principles responsible for imagining any future outside the motion pictures eighties early nineties teenaged roller boys crisscrossing a swath through a vaguely Californian apocalyptic cityscape similar in style to the way Mount Etna appears as I would write or had written this a moment ago {source: sample: overdub}, since everything worth reading is timed & everything worth writing should be a bomb

v.12.o

(You look up & see the same black birds circling the sky in wordless synchronization, the same birds you saw in Spain the summer before, the same coordinated murmuration, on the trail of Benjamin's exile & now we're turning inward you think, now it's your turn to circle the sky—gradient

v.13.o

In the French soap opera on Netflix, I am still enjoying
the pleasure of being ridden by you below the docks in
Marseilles, unbeknownst to pedestrians & street magicians
circling

v.7.2

allure & a lore & a lure

v.13.1

In a conflicting memory, a zombie is walking across the
façade of an apartment in Paris's 5th, spray-painted to the
left of the window's ledge

if you are looking at the window
in my body

v.13.2

In a conflicting memory, I am the zombie

v.13.3

In a conflicting memory, I delight myself in being sprayed
by the sea breeze on Coney Island, H a few feet away (in each
direction) shooting me in two formats

still & moving   moving &
still

v.12.1

in transition from Spain to Italy, Italy to France, France to
New York, & the mystery of birth in the air makes me always
think (as I run below it) how successful I will be or have

been as a vampire, living off of everyone I touch or have felt within me, deeply, what would it mean (I often wonder as I'm running below it) to grow still more fascinated by the disintegration of my body in relation to the decomposition of the text—on so many mornings that I've often lost count (as I run below the black birds in a Europe I would have only otherwise known from uncut novels)—whether this scene would be better colored by Madonna or Cyndi Lauper, Cyndi Lauper or Duran Duran, Duran Duran or New Order, or maybe, maybe, maybe

P
r
i
n
c
e
)

v.14.o
open on marseilles (which is
known for its soap)
tracking shot of the olive

oil bar being
lathered toward a foamy c
wave as I flesh

out exposition   vague
archives & indiscriminate
commentary   example

my fourth time
in france I learned
they don't build

a make like mine
they call this
an imported body

v.7.3
Screenplays. Screenplays. Screenplays. Screenplays.
Screenplays. Screenplays. Screenplays.

v.14.1
The image stutters until it resembles a muscle beating.
Pixelated breath or tremors, what we call a glitch is
technology's unfolding as a natural being

v.15.o
it's so hard
to imagine what
a person is
thinking I always think
you can only
put your own
stuff in another's body

v.7.4
M asks me what I live for & I tell M I live for
the enactment of mood &
the rediscovery of it (so often that
which arrives in looking
up as we read)

v.12.2
He wants submission (isn't that why we're here?); he wants,
also, to know what I call it, if I call it anything, what it's

about, where it comes from—the fiction or fetishization, I think, of an origin—& are there keywords? But he's already annotating the text, asking whether I shouldn't include instructions

v.16.o
how u likin the atlantic coast?

good to get out of paris
& have ppl
take pics of me

v.6.1
The nine hundred and thirty-seven passengers—what the news reports call "clandestinos"—will remain in Catania, for identification and processing. They will become illegal, under the law, which has no language to recognize persons who are just passing through, with no intention to settle into permanent residency within any nation. Under the law, they will become speechless and unrecognizable, incapable of being heard, of being seen

v.12.3
: migration, surveillance, self-making, fantasy, (the flow of) desire (across spaces or bodies)

v.2.1
And where does the newborn go from here? The net is vast & infinite

v.17.o
Sometimes it is necessary to invent fictions to evoke the

memory of real trauma, the possibility of telling this story again

v.18.o

Remember: any critical investigation of the edge bears the relentless task of remaking boundaries (to straddle their speculative & scopic horizons)

v.19.o

I heard the flesh
is faster than
the word   I heard

hardly anyone
thinks that
when we look

we are also always
touching an after
image (the burst

of lust that's left
to leaven)
what is the difference

or is there between
the meaty real
& the needy imaginary

the self from what the self
performs the rim of which
I've sucked to stillness

v.17.1

I am thinking about an arc of sweat just below
the collarbone, a face when its body
is about to erupt, & the eruptive breath
itself, the way the head seems to
open up & unfold like the world
against a half-held mouth, the lean in
a hip half twisted & divorced
of context by discontinuity &
misplacement they each become somehow
more intimate   in the absence of event
lies mood which is
deeper you know
before language or just coming to
language   again

v.7.5

Without references, each photograph takes on an artificial or fictional quality, & heightens the reader's sensitivity of how they might see or stand inside the scene

v.20.0

The greatest trick of capitalism wasn't making objects into money ~~it was making people into objects~~ it was making people turn ourselves into the objects we consume

v.21.0

The first time I found out I wasn't real I was transcribing these notes, "Sign Your Name" by Terence Trent D'Arby playing in the background as I energetically typed away, probably thinking of something feral because how could you not be picturing bodies stacked on bodies after that opening cue, right on the synth drum, before a human voice even kicks in, & at that moment, or maybe just before, maybe a little later, a beam of light zigzagged inside my left eye # sign your name across my heart I want you to # panicked, I placed my right hand over my right eye so I could isolate the thin sheet streaming in my left, like when a certain body or certain body parts are blurred out on the news, a scrolling strip of amber cutting across the screen, bisecting the world into two stages or levels or scenes: online shopping via our third-party provider, my relentless fervor for hand-me-down pantyhose. I rose & closed both eyes; the vibrant streak remained, light without a light source. That's how I knew it was really in me, how I knew I was neither a subject nor software but a system error, coded as noise

v.19.1
flesh is my one
constant elegy
if you were

me you'd play
this with
the windows

low

v.22.o
This sounds different than it did the last time; one hardly ever asks the text whether it isn't the user who's changed

v.23.o
I hear air
force pilots
prefer the term remote
piloted aircraft
to refer to drones

they operate, allowing
them to be
leave there is a body still
in the picture

v.24.o
the fantasy
of unlimited
duration: watching
julia roberts
cry between
the two seats
in front of me

v.25.o
(punchline to a joke I haven't written:
heyhey ordure in the court)

v.23.1

> *Monday, 25 June (13:00)*
> *New drones from wireless telecom giants could help save lives this hurricane season by providing cell phone coverage to first responders & victims of natural disasters. The FCC has already granted AT&T (NYSE: T) permission to use its flying COW (Cell on Wings) to restore cellular services, while Verizon's (NYSE: VZ) drones are still in the testing phase but will be available later this year*

v.26.o
Alternate titles for this poem include

"Self-Portrait with Phantom Twin"
&
"From the Theater of Disappearances"

v.23.2
heat seeking
something heat
can spread itself

over (more
heat) so voice
<<word missing>> or

machinic persistence
for some itinerant
expression of desire

this particular form of ache
(let's call it
an american ache)

v.17.2
I'm not after the body but what's left behind when the body
moves, when it collapses inward or elides touch   like,
how do I feel you on me, when you're not on my skin?

v.2.2
the blossoming of our duty
our beautiful every
day without
concept

no difference btw
the not yet & the already

the secret belonging
to the image
outside
its frame

(remember this
doesn't have
to mean anything)

what the hand makes
when it takes its other
hand—nature
of reversibility
& the sign

says border
control is
personal so I
duck

out & avoid
biometric
confrontation
while everything else

rises: stocks
temperatures
the sun & seas
my skin softened

& oiled to
ward the refrain
a song for myself
(a pittance)

close
in on my mouth on my breath

on the glassy
surface

adoration of the detail
absent the broker's fee

visible, divisible, assessable, storable, trans
portable & *"rationable"*

but for the sacred froth of the indirect
or misdirected indiscretion
the wetness
of certain lexical blends

in algo-rhythmic ecstasy
we are trading
futures again

as if I were the rock & their hands
were the water

relentlessly plodding
my body without pause

like rain flowing upwards
on the windshield

or runaway tears
on a crest
fallen face

a moment of pleasure be
coming eternal in memory

v.21.1
& [then] at some point as I continued to type these notes the light went [out]

v.27.o
moving always pries something open—which is me I am
pried open not by travel but by myself
in constellation of so many others
before me which might as well be
within me

like any body I too
want to be inside words
or to open them up, for each word
to show me what's inside

v.15.1
M reminds me to collage myself
in: how I feel about being desired
turned on, in control, ashamed, et cetera

auto-voyeurism, not just
the permutation of the self but the permission
& perversion / the desire to taste
the image

v.28.o
to move or be moved
by a mood / a scene / a color—desire
is always for me to make something
happen

v.15.2
the event as occasion
for an event

the interstices the straddle

the cheeks & between
the cheeks the tongue

v.27.1
would you be alarmed if I trickled
out in front of you, in the face
of shame, on the face of it
or would you find you
liked this more

v.15.3
me as subject (author); you as subject (research); me as object (desire); you as object (screen projection)

v.17.3
writing a poem is like peregrination
we walk without wanting
to know where

reading this back is like licking
the image, a second tap
to know I've been eaten

v.7.6
the body as code (digital), as codified (alluring), as coded (queer/straight) outside the body / the tension between

transmission (digital) & transmitting (cum) / the body as incorporeal vehicle

& yet to be picked up
arrested, detained

v.15.4
I like the idea of this
conversation about the text
surviving in the text

I like knowing there are always secrets
to be seeded from a given
text to be secreted from the text
to be ceded delivered laid down
turned over & always to be
waiting for one to wait for it

v.29.o
Is it or isn't it true that this repetition of movement is a method to find a form to which feeling can attach itself—like S, who felt, as consciousness is harnessed to flesh—& yet to

v.30.o
To imagine being in all the same places as you

v.29.1
slip the harness down one's waist & let the flesh feel for its own way out …

v.30.1

, to walk in the same parabola at slightly different moments
… is not to miss each other, but to invite
the other   into a space   for meeting

and the laws
that make us illegal

A photo of a photo of a photograph. Representation—doesn't it?—comes twice, or not at all. So the person behind the camera reprises the role of a stranger to this city and themselves. As a boy I used to marvel that the letters in a closed book did not get scrambled and lost overnight. He quoted that fabulous passage back in his own voice (again) as the image track vibrated across the mid-afternoon, with the sun already in its accustomed position and the shadows leaking from the windows near the double doors from where I'd entered moments ago or months. What's the difference between lingering and loitering loitering and lengthening? (the occasion for consensual encounters) Between the space of a single room and the single body within it. And the laws that make us illegal in certain parts or provinces. Don't you think the way we met is kind of unreal? Fingers grazing the thin white walls of a museum in the outskirts of some northern Italy—*the Fat One*, affectionally named for its cherished cuisine—except he hasn't eaten since this morning; except he's always hungry. Except people also say *the Learned One*. A viewer (if there ever were another one) would describe the person behind the camera as distracted or trying hard at distraction, absorption, seesaw between boredom and deep focus that allows the everyday to soften into the unfolding of an image carried across the bandwidth of a screen, the faces we put on along the lit-up corridors and boulevards. Close up, if you put your own face to the image—a man floating at the edge of a rooftop, all but the forehead, the nose and cheeks submerged in a swimming pool—maybe you'll see my own, my own facing staring back, half obscured by the mobile in my right hand, the other still grazing the thin white walls of a museum, unless (I imagine) the other is writing a caption to this artwork absent of one.

Or maybe best to wipe the image from your screen (wipe the image from your mind). Muted scatter of ripples to let the viewer know there was a body here; there were both eyes shut; there were the limbs stretched like clothes hung out to dry, reaching toward the impossible skyline of a metropolis that could be chroma keyed, empty like any good adjective. If asked to begin again, I'd write instead about the smells and sounds below, everything happening on the streets obscured from this peculiar vantage. What a time to be alone like this. What a time to be alive like this. Or maybe I'd just listen to the voice of the man selling his records in the underground intersection at Broadway and Lafayette, the warbling, uncertain intermezzo of "John Coltrane" by Billy Higgins penetrating the rush of pedestrians walking with their heads down, silently striding to the margins of this text. To relocate in other outfits, other accents and occupations, without witness.

The way books mature in being unpublished, and even more, in being unwritten. Reduced to the embryonic seed permitted by latency (the absence of composition, printing, distribution, promotion, reception, an audience, et cetera), words had begun to accumulate meaning. Like a reverse expiration, through which the numbers behind the lids of each text pointed to an uncertain but eventual arrival. Since to delay a thing—to put it on hold—is also to hold it up, allow it to ripen in the warmth of the sun and the candied eternity we call sky.

my one gift: to practice
posterity before
disappearing

So what if we happened to stop rubbing out every mistake and honored them. So the sun was actually about to set on the horizon and the man about to drown. She leaned in and whispered, now let's do something just for fun. Leaves curling in the dry depths of summer. And then we began to substitute our particles: the awe of the body reopening; to hear the sound of an evening storm moments before it ever touches the flesh, and how.

I am forgetting my first language again.

But if I hold onto that amorphous cloudiness that allows something like forgetting to take shape, something like memory. And the necessity to translate the story as I tell it. I remember another image, one I'd neither lingered over in passing nor photographed. When she'd speak, when she'd tell us a story, all of us gathered in the enriched poverty of the family room—trying to time the beats between the soft blur of the wooden fan lapsing overhead and the rocking chair's unsteady sighing—she'd interrupt the last sentence in English to say it again in Spanish, then again in Polish, before moving ahead, advancing, but at a different pace, accounting for the temporal registers of another tongue as on the lip of a secret river, each word ushering another voice and another logic into the cascade of skin and sensation, rimming the corners of the mouth.

a mouth (that can't be)

possible plot: someone comes
or someone goes

like a whole day
that will never happen

I emerged in full flower

craving blur we smear
vaseline over both eyes
again we channel
the opposite of
there is

I declare I love you
you declare the worst
part about a muffin
is dealing
with the wrapper

he offered "mechanical depth"

she craved lychees in cans
& forever glass
noodles + my unintentional special
effects

the wall opens
to become a window

the face opens
to become a hole

possibly a landfill
last ditch

effort or ill
advised destination

for everything that cannot be
reused or recycled

designed to prevent further
contamination

yet the lanky arm is leaking
blood again, a stream
of cherry flavored hi-c

as my organs long
to play
that old familiar tune

I watched them disappear
my cheek creases

feeling

envy for the secondhand
tempo of stepping out

to share a cigarette
give me something to do

outside myself

absorb
each drag

& resuscitate
old memories
in new bodies

they were “famous” for hating onions
he had auditioned to be my “script girl”

I watch my cockles
undergo an untrained
extraction in my mobile
memory

still rehearsing my part
from a passed down
recipe: to write

as though the words are being translated from another tongue

(in the right
light his face looked
like prepackaged
parfait)

the “pounding regularity”
of form curdling
a diverse field of signifiers

we too were (there)
reenacting the original
sin on my potential
lowboy

the pulp of consciousness
juicing into words

what is the difference btw
sweeping & scraping
scraping & scanning

the mingling of fantasy
memory
banal
extraordinary
calling into question the frames of the narrative's "reality"
→ make this plausible

gathering material about the hand's relationship to stone

one's mind is elsewhere:

(an explanation or defense of the camera technique that
allows an audio track to infiltrate an unrelated image track)

the lush cadence
of nonsynchronous sound

mesmerized by euclidean
rhythms I ate

my flaky hand
pie pressed

against plaka promenade
dumpster (everything

sold on sight)
admire only

the extended
j-cut & its use

fullness in the past
as for our presence

they measured my marvelous
lengths with five hands

& planted (on my person)
a warning or prophecy

clean your iphone before it's too late

people also ask: what does it mean to be on the sales floor?

what you're witnessing is a video being copied to a vhs tape,
that tape being digitized, & then that digitized video being
copied onto the tape again (the process is repeated a total of
sixteen times)

as sensual as vegetables
being jet-sprayed
at the supermarket

as sensual as bushes
shaking in the morning breeze

asking with your eyes vs. asking with your mouth

(there's something savory in eastern philosophy)

not fond of classifications
call me whatever you wish
so long as you keep feeding me
clean rivers, lakes, & streams

circling the brink of canal
drawn to the death of our faces
in every storefront's gaze
a haircut is the least of my concerns

but arouse my quantum state
in this sam goody
reorganizing the shelves
according to volume

I graph your black hole & externalize our abstract urges
film / body / dream
+ the repetition of [cut] as if montage

anything to make our ends
meet, practicing
quality conversation like

what's the weather & is there traffic
chanting

some of my fave-uh-rit words are ,,,

watermelon
gentlemen
bread
bicicleta

(swelling electronic music)

"seemingly overnight"

automated voiceovers overlaid
with footage of people squeezing
clay from one palm to the other

SEO debris
keyword salad

honing methods for deepening
the void instead
of filling it

since real
tears flow

though keep rewinding
until all we can see
glittery ribbons
of static

claiming booty
in the bonus round

what is the dirtiest orifice
in the human body

hint: it's not
what you would think

calves tensing
midway through cloud
forest walk
to seek
a greedy vista

(river's absent
body beneath

the darkened bronze)
in lieu of flowers

compare the cost
of my unswerving
postnasal drip
with downtown congestion
pricing

my only sin: sin
vergüenza
to exist without
the possibility
of shame

after all I am
your large language model

they will have been
throbbing
for my unannounced catwalk

(I meant extraordinarily meaty
in a good way)

but you are not
your leg warmers

& disgust evolved
from fear of
animals that want to
eat you from the outside

16 actors that share the same face
4 signs you have fungus in your gut

(she was sending me, but I don't know where)

"a form of excess, like a mouth that can't be closed"

does calling it home make it so

of all the lessons I ignored since childhood, the greatest
one was the idea that I should keep anything
to myself

what is the difference btw being haunted & being hunted?

(identity is to realism as alterity is to desire)

a conviction that language & meaning
are porous & lack clear boundaries

an ethical commitment to riffraff

overlap & intersection, not
equivalence & similarity

memo to students:
"no casual excursions in the archive"

with the vivacity & abandon of someone eating a mango
with two hands, I tongued [   ]

why the need to say "I" here?

a witness to authorize your fantasy
which authorizes mine

so cosign your name
across my heart

& shed our stains
by keyhole

readying this tornado
of affection

our aspiration to fashion
an air quote

from an unembellished
ass cheek quick

sand my greatest
fear in the nineties

or how birds sound
from a fifth floor

apartment
perturbed

by a nervous radiator
parallel

story in which
I am wolf

-ing half
a dozen

cardamom buns
necromancing

the route taken
by the staten island ferry

when staten island
is no longer

once upon a time we were

come once then
come again

divine aura of reincarnation

she claims buddhism
pays dividends

time of the taco < tacotime
-'s handrolled crisp
burritos

(it's a difference
you can taste)

so they say
later / offstage

ugh love
seeing
your green dot

dolly shot above columbia
river gorge

would you know I want every hole in me
to be both loaded & flushed

would you know I want to read any text as if it is a book of spells, as if just copying out the words—mouth to mouth—could transubstantiate language & literature into life, but better, because it's been passed through another

true ruin

But now is not then. If then ever was a now.

My ghost image / floating / the right radio waves / your screen, me spliced into smaller versions and reconditioned as code, to be yours now or your now, to be you now, again and again and again, a temporal kink whose digital discharge powers the erotics of indeterminacy. What can never be arrived at, in spite of an incessant search: entanglement without timeline; a torso without edges; a life without history.

Interminable scrolling trades linearity for loss, loss for memory, anticipation, immediacy, immediate presence. Continuous and customizable frames zoomed in and cut into, cropped closer, each detail exploding into the primary image. Tell me to keep going, since in the distance, you say, is the redemption of the periphery: indistinct gradations of black that rim the stuff inside a coffee cup and the night sky and the propped up backside and the curtain at the cinema that rises to reveal not a moving picture but another curtain of the same or similar shade, that makes me search, digits gliding over a toolbar: *upon what does a shadow depend?*

My message interjects; your screen, once fingered, gleams with another ghost image: discrete events enwrapped in digital sheen, where dislocation brings us closer to a mobile center from which we hone our desire. Whatever it is I have sent to you, whatever I have said or shown to you, says (without saying anything), *join me here and now in this want*. To be here, repeat, and to be now, and thus, to be redundant. An excess that registers the fact that all of this is nevertheless non-indexical. Having been here is now there. If being ever was akin to having, if we ever even had anything. Didn't you know. My body (too) projected like that (on the palm) is a poem (dorsal and pulverized) to be reconstructed against the ratio of the real thing (afforded by the proxy of arousal), each click unfolding, not a beginning, but the continuation of encounter that has never stopped occurring.

I return to your message so I can return to presence. Like walking out from the dark of the crowded theater into the daytime of the crowded city to discover that nothing has changed except the lighting. Stripped of source, every subject-object exceeds its medium. Larger than life but no bigger than 6.1 inches. Surrender looms in the hunt. A cascade of skin with captions in place of signatures, an autograph that would otherwise tether a copy to its original. I like this body; I swipe this body. But the point isn't substitution; it's displacement, it's synchronicity. Because *the reality we are making now is not the time of narrative*. Not, you sound back, a narrative of time. All you can eat and around the clock. I want us to keep nibbling, for fear of losing our hunger. The way the flesh rests on the white coverlet or sheet. And the dark strip linking tuft to taint. I want to hold on to it, but I could also let it bob and drift. I could also lie down; I could also lay myself down to admit some tendons weren't made for names. True ruin. A sacrifice tempered by my stream, the hushed refrain of unbroken flow. Then mime my exit theme. Say: *the air traveling through the instrument cleans the whistle* as a lyric hum. Whenever it is I'll be done writhing. Even the crystalline orbs that rise only to die at the lip of the highball I cup in one hand as I am doing this (with the other) ease their afterlife into an account that has not yet hardened. The throb at the top of the very top of the muscular tube inside the neck voices my desire. I will swallow what I have to, because I have to. Since all absence desires to be endlessly repeatable.

I touch (myself), I keep touching, not because I want to feel (myself) or even be felt, not because I want to remember the body, not because I want a reminder of the body but because I want to escape this, to forget (myself), to have forgotten the fact of a past or the idea of having a future, and when I think to look (to look back), I find you, too, are nowhere to be found. Dead, maybe, not gone.

delay to penetrate
(notes on trash)

what if you could see the air your family breathes in your own home? what would you see? how would you feel?

(I'm on hold with the a/c repair)

is it my air conditioner that is defective or the air I breathe?
the air I breathe or my body?

when I want to infuse my everyday with drama, I turn on local traffic. there's always a breakdown. things are happening all the time & every time it happens suddenly. the voices of the faces we will have to imagine keep talking about "alternates," about "approaches," "blocks," "crashes," "jams." I want the language of delay to penetrate me, & thus invade this text

(I'm still on hold)

people fond to drop
in at my doorstep
without warning

they wanted the knock
off version

but an address
can always be changed
in secret

she asks what do you pack
if you don't know you're never coming back

he had a "borderline disorder"

pricked by the punctum of two cocks
crowing
instead of the expected one

like an AI photograph
I contain multitudes

then we took turns
massaging one another
in "bullet time"

then we sifted through my unopened male
until I recognized letters
I'd never taken in till now

wanting you with bangs with cufflinks with jeans torn
into jean shorts

they tried to read it with a "straight face"
then they read me very gay

after boarding we watch if looks can
kill
          I verified my identity
          with a series of one
          time codes

hold on with confidence
says the sign on the staircase
of my favorite escalator

(they'd asked me to give a 10 min talk on the differences
btw getting felt up & getting touched up)

I wanted "free
napkins" but the automatic
toilet dispenser offered
only "free tampons"

upending karl's simple circulation
of commodity trade expressed

as a triplet of variables

(to wit: a gratis ditty)

so that night desires
rain from an aisle
seat & sanitized
calm of pre

packed animal already
lasered into potential
mouthfuls my torso
flipped

again & reinserted
since I tape
even latent experience
could I watch myself as we

commit to hold
the audio near
despite a gap
in form (frenzy

of a humming on
the record) sometimes
forgotten as one tracks
my reluctance to pump

breath back into the shaft
like a head
of lettuce dreaming
as it lies in garden's

darkness looking up
at the half moon synthetic
fleece over each
thigh question or command

to skim syntactical
arrangement of parts
of speech I triangulate
digital sweat / crumbs / & my lack

of oxford commas as
a dark film begins
to harden against our clean
& plastic purchase

another cruising
altitude or emptiness
of the adriatic if the sun
continues its march

back in the capital of the twentieth century
or: at home at the end of the world

here I am watching jimmy
carter memes on repeat

what's the difference between being memorable &
remembered remembered & immemorial

my boss's misreading of foucault
masqueraded
as "a big idea"

we are leaving the american
sector we are leaving the self
checkout with our dumpy reusable

grocery bags in tow to muddle
a spatial-temporal order
& the border between

bodies without which one
can just as suddenly become
the other

(he "cried" over
spilled "milk")

but I slide this turtle
neck over the arms

I've asked
to raise above the head

what does it mean (for you) if I call it my "favorite sweater"?

what does it mean if I say coming back instead of going back
going back instead of leaving? since return—isn't it?—is not
listed among any of our possible scenarios

then we proceeded from the glitch & passed the error
into actuality

with reptilian focus he mouthed
the words that were merely
background music

what are your inward-facing practices?

I am asking my students, but also asking myself: how do you
find ways to be with yourself & for yourself? what are the
things you produce without thinking about being productive?

plants produce glucose & oxygen
slugs produce mucus
spiders produce silk
my ten-month-old produces wet diapers

what's the difference between a durable good & a nondurable
good a nondurable good & the permanence of airpods
beneath our scorched soil

"rough estimate":
each person every day in the united states produces
4.9 pounds of municipal solid waste

what does my trash say about me? maybe at the very least the privilege of keeping trash, of consuming things, of holding a body that carries other things other bodies or the flesh they once belonged to

+ the literal cost of the privilege: one hundred & fifty dollars every quarter for a person or people to drive by once a week, collect my trash, deposit it with everyone else's

I like to think of the moment my trash mingles with my distant neighbors', each of our traces strangers to each other & ourselves. there, under cover of dawn, we gather in our decrepitude, in our tendency to rot, in our desires to be absorbed, for our identities to be flattened, for our selves to disintegrate

a student says an onion that is named lovingly will grow taller than an onion that was called harmful things

though I can't remember their name

a betrayal of language or memory memory or naming ,,, ?
the betrayal of being named

when I was a child I'd ride with mom to the town recycling center marveling at the meticulous organization of what's already been used & consumed papers here plastics there glass around the bend. (each time I gleefully chucked a bottle of snapple mint tea into the bin reserved for glass, I thought about how these objects would soon assume a different life once they've been discarded & because they've been discarded, that in order to be redeemed they'd have to be abandoned, that saving requires a certain violence, that to give something a name is also to forget it & forgetting begins in memory)

it felt, when I was still a child, so simple, so easy, to be honored with a new life, a new shape, a new self, which wasn't meant to be forever, since nothing is forever

(his mind was all made up)

they asked me if I ever heard of god, and I answered that I even saw movies, for adults. I know exactly how this ends

l'eclisse

1

A refusal is offered. A frenzy is tolerated. The promise of total darkness for two minutes and forty-one-point-six seconds. I am born.

2

Desire = to leave [behind] a story, where story = unrepeatable existence
+ the notion of distance intervening

3

Consider that all links to an assumed nativity are broken prior to birth. So exile short-circuits the trajectory of "plot" for the children who emerge from its arhythmic pitch. (And in the margins: Cut the hedge between *presentable* and *present.*)

We might as well be anywhere < We're in "the middle" of nowhere

4

When I want to play exhibitionist and voyeur—and when do I ever not want both and at the same time?—I ride.

5

(I came from the conjugations of *flight.*)

6

Born of the desire to look but also to be looked at and in a way that I can control, while relinquishing control. To make sense of that slippery paradise—somewhere between representation and expression, I am about to be born on the page (estoy en proceso; listen for the shutter as exposure kicks in)—I want to remind myself (by repeating it here) that to author is to transfer; to move words and images around.

7
The good side versus the bad side (of every face awaiting exposure in a photograph). Skin has a kind of volume that can and cannot be adjusted. Liquid, too, tastes different depending on the vessel. (Notion of being a "sucker," or to put myself in another's mouth.) I always eat well, a friend says. Another friend says I always eat meals at their correct times. Everyone at their assigned stations awaiting another eclipse. Whenever I perform this exercise, I neglect the rules. I am not, nor have I ever (I like to sometimes add) aimed for exactitude.

8
The time of the image and the time of the sound. Which comes first?

9
There are things I don't understand about myself, and to write is not to bring me anywhere closer to a truth but instead to relish the impossibility of a certain self-knowledge … my need to be dazzled as a spectator, not to look in myself or at myself but to offer up myself as a sight to behold. Even if it is only me who is looking.

10
And then again, to write is always to want to read together; to want to read together and to be together in all of our unknowable difference. (The plural space of appearance.)

11
If asked to describe my impaired vision, I'd call it *sparkle sight*. Glitter explodes against surfaces whose uniform color I used to take for granted. I am cut open, along with the world, where every object breathes, where every breath is confetti, where light performs as soul, or an optical equivalent, and I am everything I thought I'd wanted.

stripped of index
like a memory relocated

in the split
of east/west

12
At what point, he wondered, does the body begin to eat itself?

9b. [restored from the damaged original]
The appropriate medium here is video (whether or not actual video is utilized): video as rehearsal

In the background: Revise the notion of reversibility between *looking* and *being* (for all those who have had to learn to hide behind our eyes). How to hold—without reconciling—the private activity of the public act? Produce a channel to which a reader-viewer might flow.

(flow as a system of feeling)

The text (any text) arrives somewhere between documentable presence and perishable trace. I collect sounds, sensations. Haven't you ever mistaken someone else's gaze for your own? A writer is a faulty recorder. We play things back with difference.

13
People will shoot flaming arrows in the sky to try to rekindle the sun. Others will immerse themselves in rivers up to their necks. I tell my students to produce a déjà vu in the text by staging the interval, not of the occurrence between two dissimilar things (example: light/darkness) but of their disappearance as singular.

14
(I read that R, who goes by many other names, sips the nectar of immortality and is, each time, beheaded before he can swallow it.)

15
The intersection between autobiography and biography desires an "I," but an I, nevertheless, that is multiple, susceptible, obscured, transparent. To be behind me as we do this is to have a view of the scraps. Or the cuts begged by the flesh itself: the prostheses I've tried on and abandoned.

16
Notion of the *close second*, which I want to say is also an experience of writing (an experience of reading) that is nothing if not "in your face."

17
Did I mean *story* or did I mean *life*?

18
(The promise of total darkness for two minutes and forty-one-point-six seconds.)

I don't want to tell you what I already know; I want to find out what I don't. Or intensify the cavity through sensitive lineation (a possible response to my neighbor's question: *So like, what is a poem?*).

Ontological restlessness countered by aesthetic rather than epistemological interventions.

19
In a dream, I wake to write down details of the film before it comes to an end, without acknowledging that the film ends when I wake to write it down.

What was your experience of that? Of being both and between? I feel like whatever this is, I reply, it's a wish to hold onto the friction of passing, the noise that isn't meant to be patched as signal.

(A lingering close-up betrays the notion that the lightweight, handheld camera has gone unnoticed.)

20
Are you waiting, like me, for the moment when juxtaposition turns into absolute proximity (absolute approximation), when identification with another and identification of the other (as irremediably unlike any other) are not antagonistic but coordinate?

21
I mask.

I am masking.

I have masked.

I have been masking.

I masked.

I was masking.

I had masked.

I had been masking.

I will mask.

I will be masking.

I will have masked.

I will have been masking.

22
evidence is presented → the truth begins to take
shape

like a character who undergoes
recasting in the middle
of the scene

No difference between living it and making it (for all those who have had to first create a past to which we can return).

23
I want to remember to describe the lit-up windows as the F rolled on (as it does, three or four times an hour, even in the beats before dawn), the passengerless amber of each train's compartment as it appears from the bedroom, where a fan loops idly over my head. Think of the opening of *L'eclisse*. The difficulty of repeating certain things by heart and still this desire to do it and my whole life to do it. Three minutes (maybe more, I haven't exactly counted) of watching a fan blow across a nondescript Roman studio, or what I imagine to be a studio in Rome in the years before life began, by which I mean a time before I was born and my parents were just children fleeing the violence they nevertheless could not name. (Some of this occurs off screen.) A beautiful literary translator splits from their writer boyfriend, only to meet a lively trader on the unsteady floor of the stock exchange. In this scenario, I would like to assert my candidacy to play two of the three major roles. The task of the translator is to guess which.

24
Because I can never tell myself.

hypothesis of the leather jacket

Have you ever been told *you are different in person*?
Different in words? Language, too, is a screen

drawn to the (porosity)
of big bodies

Like meat becoming sausage, the long, dull hug of non-recognition; face up against the mirror; palm over cheek; cheek on tongue, or the reverse. Played back, I want to insert a set of keys & a glass of pop on the counter, the swift translucent pearls & the sound of edging, a clapping in the grass if you found a tape deck stashed under the bush. The (remaining) inches being latent

Want to source the etymology of "applause"; the torso tending to eruption, as when body-mind aspires to slush; consciousness susceptible to mutation, thrust, seepage. A renegotiation of place, in which body is or has been held

here I am again
reading benjamin on the side
walk, a view of the gated
park, if I were looking   all the legs
darting in the periphery
gestures I've seen
in other films   I write
back   I like
the idea of passersby
fancying me
a trick

I want to be true, but I also want to retain the excess & curiosity of being invented

Place (parentheses) around otherwise innocuous adjectives

an aspect of language closer
to consciousness

today when
there is no such thing
as celebrity even
as each one of us
plays publicist

Describe the discrepancies, or the instances when *I* & *the author* converge

algebra & the reunion
of parts (a miraculous flowering
of calligraphers follows
any disappearance
of the prophet)

hypothesis of the leather
jacket, a banquet
feast, the ritual of
plunging face
first into this chalice

"If writing is the dramatization of language which duplicates in visual terms"

Since meaning is revealed if & when the words are copied out, since to author is to transfer, since to transfer requires a witness to consecrate the text; drama of being alive or of becoming living

(A boom mic amplifies your dictation; my eyes crush a broth of tears)

Notion of the slush fund, the slush pile, the iconic, authentic brand offering an extensive array of illicit, unsolicited goods

& services (white canine, blue shirt, red slush puppie) passed on at one's pleasure

I want to be informal & half-cocked, but I also want to have the liberty to attain rhythmic "high points"

When the camera jammed as the author's home ignited, we, the fastidious crew, were tasked with rebuilding the house, to burn it again

Do you prefer to absorb or to be absorbed? Vapor paste or skin. Beaten (like slush) into indiscrete meat, perfume of the hips, the thighs, the "back matter" that plays at description & summary, an attempt to grasp, seize, or otherwise penetrate (the text)

Remember? Earthen vessels were in universal use in antiquity (they are twice mentioned in the New-ish Testament), & their broken fragments, which could be picked up almost anywhere, were made to serve (various purposes)

Upon the smoothest of these pieces of unglazed pottery, the poorest among us might write our memoranda, receipts, letters, or wish lists of the bodies we'd like to be inside

reaches permitted

so reality comes & be
comes more & more
vivid more &
more unreal

What exists behind the face? We took turns with our hands, seeing who could slide the emptied pint glass closest to the edge of the counter without making it drop. You asked again & I said more. More what? More face. I wanted to say but didn't say it. We each waited for the shriek that follows any fall, every fall. We would each keep waiting. Wanting, at the same time, to melt into the Hong Kong evening until we were no longer persons playing a bar game but the cigarette smoke dusting the hazy beach club in summertime, watching all the others in their vibrant bathing suits & unbuttoned short-sleeved shirts, the sleeves soft and thin, & the sweat marks that patterned the shape of the bodies beneath, as if from the beneficial perspective of a treasured divan. Like suburban New Jersey. Face, I repeated, as you downed another mug of crystalline beer & I watched the sailboats cast off, but it was night now, & there was no wind, no sailboats, no bodies beneath. Face, I repeated, maybe this time aloud, from the Latin facere: to make, to do. My face is being made; it is doing things; it is not yet done, et cetera. Case in point: My face undergoes another arrangement without consulting me, without my approval; face first, as they say, a natural fact.

The way the domed glass slides across the cool granite countertop & the sound that one object makes against the other reminds me of the hot stones on my fist-beaten back, the way the anonymous palms place each volcanic orb on my brown skin with provident attention & measureless intensity, the beauty & terror of the unseen arrangement. A face, I heard, is nonfiction without consent, from the Latin verb to feel. Like almost everything, I am taking this from another tongue. Maybe I meant *nonfiction without content.* My face, right now, can't speak or remains unwilling: tongue in cheek.

Here we go again, I remember saying, unless it was you mouthing a line mimed from someone else's memory. Another round, another nonchalant plunge, the things we agree to do on a dare, our idolatry of an audience. Persons I've never seen before making ovals in their floral drinks with their plastic straws, the articulated end bending toward each throat, the obscured teeth & tongue. I put my money where your mouth should have been, the thin slit that offers the grace of temporary effacement. Here we go, you said, & I wondered whether victory meant motoring to the farthest reaches permitted by the polished surface or whether it meant hurtling beyond its material tipping point, the expectations or assumptions of a terminus, where fear dies into desire, or the reverse. I wondered if the point of our game wasn't actually to lose, since every loss begets a newfound urge to take in. Maybe also: to take out, take the place of, forgetting in the span of another muscled thrust that we were only watching it happen. And in your head, he recited these words: The boundaries of expression are the boundaries of the line. One single line. A wrinkle, perhaps, rift in space time or facetime, the hollowed tension of a prolonged smile. Plus the sigh of loose cash fished from a hip pocket & placed into a jar. Remember that I show this image so that I might withdraw myself from view. The voices, meanwhile, around us grew louder, the buzz & chatter of extras vying for air or exposure, the unnatural volume of audio that indicates this has already been dubbed & retouched.

(And each time you enter the text, the image empties out, the warm jet evacuating the warm flesh. Divide the distance & call it a story.) Adjusting one's eyelids & eyelashes & the calm part of the eyeball in order to absorb the face staring back, apprehended by the glass or the gaze behind it. Didn't you know. The face is here (there) to be used. So I relocate to the registers of the voice to the time of listening. They say my favorite color is purple & I like to dance. They say I like a party if I can get lost in it. That it's the emptiness of vast things that makes life so bearable. They say, they say. When I no longer want to be looked at, I shut my eyes.

picture the arrière-garde

in dream sweats or spasms

a minute or more
diminishes

so a raindrop
solidifies
my namesake

across a "public
surface" / on the other
line my fingers

curling the cords
on the telephone I wish
were fusilli

Remember the feeling of plastic encasing the copper cables. Remember the cord that once connected me with that breathing body that was also mine. If this is a text, it's an array of natural skin regimens and cosmetics designed for all skin and underarm types. Confusing numbers for sounds and sounds for colors (9 harbors orange qualities; 8 invites the emergence of purple). So parse the idiosyncrasies of underarms, or enumerate an accurate typology. Everyone wants to know (and so I hold my index here & click):

ARE ARMPIT PADS RIGHT FOR YOU?

There are things that need doing, things that need to be done. Notion of being "behind" on things. To be behind things. Picture the arrière-garde, who prefers to advance from the rear.

In some embodiments, the headwear insert maintains structural integrity after at least five iterations of machine-washing and after at least five iterations of machine-drying.

Things leak only if you generate the conditions necessary for inadvertent experience. Notion of the shy faucet.

What I want to explain to the committee is the wet mimetic streets strobed with alternating patterns of red green & yellow. What I want to explain to the committee is an affinity for feigning ignorance about my potential to wander. Trying to determine the specific moment pleasure becomes a substitute for desire.

Someone places a phone call and I pick up.

I say I wish I could but I can't. I say yeah yeah yeah (in quick succession, just like that. And I nodded). I say but what else are snacks for? The click of heels or dial tone.

In some embodiments, the headwear insert maintains substantially the same external width, length, thickness, and radius of curvature dimensions, each dimension within an error range of ± 15%, but preferably within an error range of ± 5%, before the five iterations of machine-washing and the five iterations of machine-drying as after the five iterations of machine-washing and the five iterations of machine-drying.

What is not clear (to me) is what my namesake says on the street corner when I approach them, wearing eyeglasses and a backpack in another book, each of us held at stoplight. Turn yellow turn red. Genetic recollection of circling Warsaw at dusk to towel my tan skin under the Malecón. Naked and the wind blows softly but it blows. A palm leaf below my bending joints for this joy of being homophonic with you. If receipts rifted from my jeans back pocket provide certain instructions:

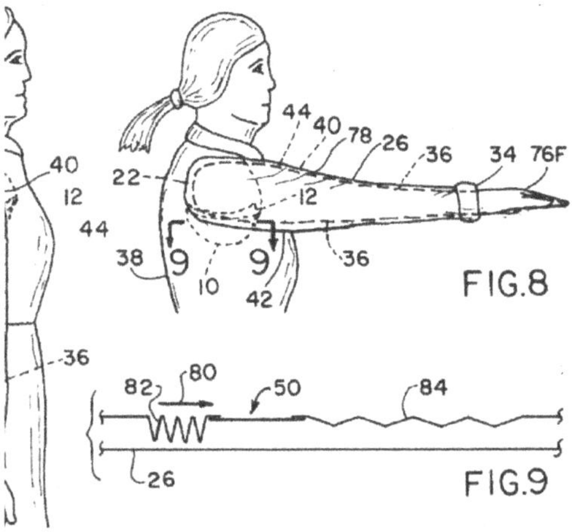

FIG.8

FIG.9

Polka dots are a unique fashion of art that people either love or hate, a student volunteers. It could be today just as well as tomorrow. The dots are boring, she says. She says, I do not buy anything with polka dots, white or black dots. Though I really like the black spots on the bodies of the ladybugs. Could it be psychological? The ladybug represents good luck and fortune. Poem that begins I want to …

In some embodiments, the seam removably couples the polyester mesh layer and the neoprene layer together.

My favorite seat on the subway train is the one nearest the train's edge, from where I can see the draw hooks connecting each car in a curving line and the jostling of each compartment as I relate this experience into memory. Stuttering cadence of assemblage, which provides the tempo for this composition.

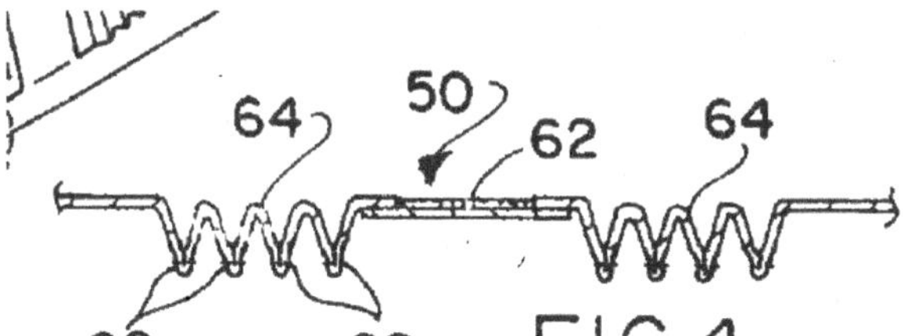

FIG.4

Is this an array of cosmetics or a two-way window? Witness the passed-down notion of "writing independently" ... silly fiction of the "independent thought." I sat here all this time, hovering between street and sky, all the time relying upon the originality of others to tell me about myself and what I'm like.

Still deciding whether to resist or absorb today's floating boredom on the F train. Today's floating anxiety and loneliness. Several undeserved sunsets on a grid and my adolescent jerk-off fantasies behind the vertical silence of blinds. Every sound associated with an object, space, person, and the things we did together. What is it to only miss things in memory.

Dial up modem & dial tone. The V train. Voicemail and automatic rewinders. Phone booths, pocket change, collect calls, the cue sticks I'd learned to balance between forefinger and thumb, incorrectly. How D would place the cue in my hand from behind, and how he'd move my bent arm (back and forth back and forth back and forth) until I felt ready to push. And the faltering gesture I produced when I did decide to release the stick with enough pressure to fling the white orb into any other. Half a dozen lizards at any given time ogling us in the Florida room, watching from the tiled floor or the pastel walls, where they climbed to get a better view of the balls spinning toward collision and the felt of the table that served as our arena. And behind us players and reptilian spectators the smell of charcoal on the barbecue that remained, and the warm wind that carried other smells too: plátanos on the frying pan laced with ajo picado y cebollas; stunted grass that pricked the undersides of my feet and the palms of my hands, so quick was I, nevertheless, to want to rub my flesh against each synthetic blade and soak up the discrepancy between real & fake; gasoline for the lawnmower D worked by pulling the rope start once twice three times; splashes of chlorine that dried against the cotton fabric of our shorts and skin without fully dissolving and the sweet fragrance ferried by a single mango tree; the dying sun and the way the sliding screen doors patterned our faces in a grid as we each were draped in shadows. I keep D's voice with me in that room, among those shadows & the chlorine dreams and my heart, preferring this skipping record to anything stored in the repositories of digital data or printed film. The daily prayer of deliverance; milkmen & paperboys. The sound of yourself crying, as a baby.

In some embodiments, hook and loop fasteners are disposed along one or more portions of the seam.

Because I want to insist on non-relations, or forge them (and so make these orphaned subjects kin), I'll reference the water buffalo who, half-eaten, dragged itself to safety when a pride of lions began to fight over its remains.

Who among us hasn't been the water buffalo? Who among us hasn't been the lion?

please
consume by
3:50pm

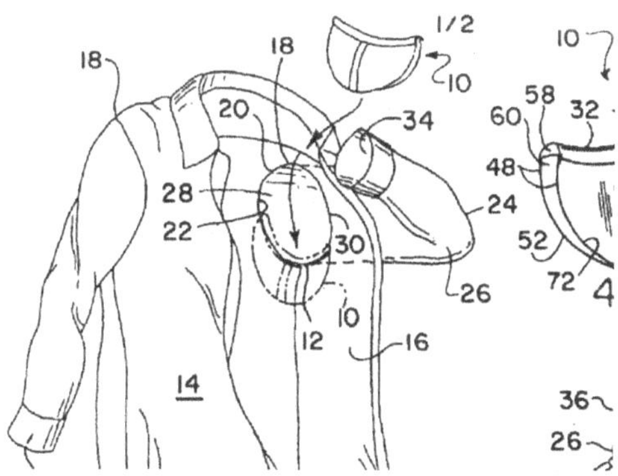

I want to take my vitamins. I want to make the fatal error message disappear. I want to be presentable. I want to listen to Grace Jones and Depeche Mode and shimmy my feet as my legs bob under the table. I want to eat well and sleep more. I want to start taking my dreams seriously. I want to resist the impulses of the poetic, excusing myself for my tendency to romanticize a silk shirt draped against the back of a desk chair, clothes without bodies, bodies without subjects, subjects without form …

(Naturally flavored with other natural flavors.)

how the light
flickers on only
after a body

passes underneath
each bulb opening
like tulips

in the archive

since not knowing
is also desire since

desire is also permission
for the breeze

to devastate me
knees pressed

against a back
in resistance / his

favorite part

of the day: when
sky holds moon

& sun
in the same

position / unspecified

length of lower
leg glistening
in pixelated

ribbons to wonder
whether one favors satin
or a glossy

finish the vapid
lacquer applied
to each orbital plate

before mounting

mute sound space
between wanting to

be me & wanting

to be mine
each muscular breath

draped in taffeta
like pudding
on a parachute

now my windows look

out onto a swimming pool. There were trees here, and with the trees, shadows, just last week. And then a week became a year and a year becomes a lifetime. The shadowless pool, and the windows one looks from, whose perspective allows the opportunity to enjoy a range of satisfactions.

Like placing the shadows back on the image track, or bathing in a bunny outfit in the deep end.

I like writing like I like a costume party. The choice to try things out, to surprise yourself in the company of people you know and nevertheless cannot recognize, or the reverse. The skin cracks under extreme pressure.

In some embodiments, a user structurally manipulates the polyester mesh layer and the neoprene layer to removably couple the polyester mesh layer and the neoprene layer.

(grab 3k of my pixels
& pull)

I'm taking a ride with my best friend. What if you pick me up on this F train. What if I deny you a fancy dinner. Bitter Italian soda pop your electrical signal on a wire. In a video, I place my face up against the plastic surface, to get a better look at the conductor who decides when we stop and when we go when we stop and when we go when we stop and when we go. And if not the conductor, who? Fictional characters & their actual feelings.

… I want to join those men in neon green jackets who scale the side of the neighboring building. I want to learn the rules of proper harnessing. I want to follow harness etiquette. I want to remember to say thank you, to no one in particular, and myself.

What's your name? she asks. Reinaldo, I say. Reinaldo Reynoso, which has a pleasing relationship to sound and space. When I say "Reinaldo Reynoso," I go gaga for staccato backroom wherewithal, the way letters rub up against each other in this verbal grind.

Maybe it feels good for you too. This carnival of bodies that are really "just words."

Understanding that there is always a hole in the image & that water remembers a thing like breath. A thing like rock & sand.

Let the silent spaces within a song rush in.

Moving through days with the knowledge that faces which do not conform to the schema fashioned by environment & experience & the morphologies of racialization can only be perceived in parts.

In some embodiments, the planar multilayered substrate comprises a bottom portion having a shape conforming to an inner lip of a headwear article.

So what are you then? Something between being not enough in some places & too much in others. Plus a long pause, breathless but for the stuttering cry that drips from my throat. Then J wants to know why I write so often, as if it were a choice between writing things down & letting life go by, as if I were only here to be here, here and only here. The hiss black spots & crackling throughout the film's entire 129 minutes were intentional.

He thinks how it's different when our fingers are interlaced than when they aren't & how he prefers holding hands to an arm around the neck or an arm, so much lower, at his side. And this remembering. And this is remembering. (Tedious motion of plot coming in again.)

Catalog a series of firsts, & the spaces in which they occurred. Catalog a series of lasts before they happen, & the spaces in which they would occur.

In a photograph or moving image memory, the mist-driven alleyways of a northwestern city in North America, foghorns in the distance and crowds gathering at market at the appointed time, puddles on the cobblestone reflecting the low-lit sky. When she waves her hand from across the street, I can't tell if she is greeting an acquaintance, or erasing their image.

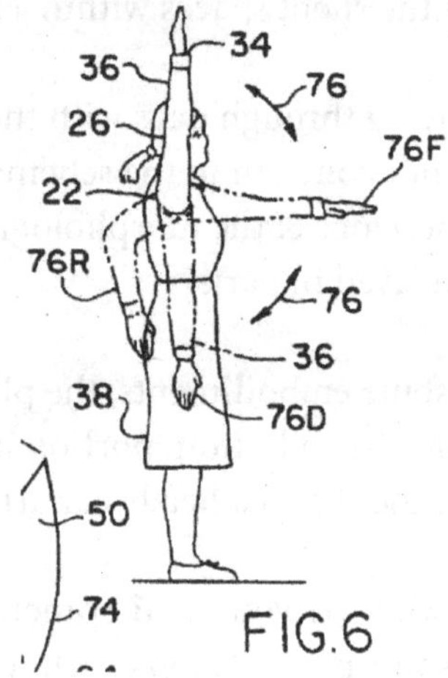

FIG.6

And is it or isn't it true that a delay doesn't cease movement but creates it?

Reinaldo Reynoso is the name of the person whose mail I receive every week, sometimes every other day, so frequently that I myself begin to mistake Reinaldo for me, unless it's the other way around. Reinaldo Reynoso, whose mail remains unopened in my lobby, on the lone table established for messages such as those contained within the white envelopes addressed to him, bearing my address. Messages that await a hand that isn't mine but could be.

In the same photo, they circled Oaxaca City before dusk on bicycles, tracing a route they knew by heart until they were each below the fabled green haven. What comes first, the memory or the experience? Whenever he met someone he wanted to remember, instead of taking a photo, he'd place the recorder on a smooth surface, or raise it, like a flickering candle, holding its shell against the flesh, and ask them to record their voice. When I think about her now, I feel a feeling like a paperclip digging underneath my skin.

Trick of the eye or a camera. What appears to be a swimming pool is a city street; what appears to be a bathing ritual is a publicity strategy for aspiring influencers. Buddha said if I don't descend into hell who will? This commercial for *The Bachelor* promises big explosions, big romance, and big reveals. Zoomed in, one might make out two animals kissing against a loading dock. Maybe there are others, awaiting the opportunity of a close crop, to permit the uncertain explosion of detail into this composition. What is more electric than the meeting of screen and skin.

still in our seats we crawl
to the next station

He was telling him that story again about the woman who, after surviving the camps, came home to the husband who no longer recognized his wife, her face being so disfigured that it required surgical restoration. What does it mean to resemble yourself, from the perspective of someone who is not you? The husband takes his wife for a stranger, someone who could pass for the person he had married, but only under certain conditions—mannerisms and gestures he would have to teach her; cadences of speaking and walking she would have to learn. So I set out to become the person others thought I was.

Was this a mistake, I think now three decades more or less later. Have I been mistaken?

When I try to picture her, there is a hole, like a space cut out from the image, where her face was, where her face would be. The task I think or one of them is not to write the image but to write the hole.

I prefer my hair unwashed. I prefer polka dots to a flannel pattern. I prefer the text to smuggle typos in publication. Tokens of use, residues of the unreliable body, the body made porous with age and invitation. Inexcusable like time.

When I got my new face, I said, they never told me I'd inherit the memories that passed before it.

the juxtaposition of foam

What does it mean to dream in another language? In another body?

J says he counts in Spanish. Sometimes I can hear him whispering the numbers when I walk into the kitchen, when I walk in from outside and all the languages I come from or belong to or don't I.

In a dream I am photographed and at the moment of exposure —moments or days later—I see another face on my body, another body on a face that isn't mine. At a certain age I stopped being able to distinguish what had happened to me in dreams and what had happened to me when I was awake.

Speed of the internet versus the delay of real life. I always think everything that will arrive will arrive whether or not we are around to wait for it. Or maybe I'm just thinking about it now because I'm waiting. There is a certain pleasure in concentration and volume and the exchange of things and bodies, and then there is traffic, the marketplace for a sensitive awareness. Involuntary attentiveness. A delay is something I aspire to; something I want to re-create: life as a continuous series of intervals.

Can you return to a place you've never been? Concept project for a future memory. In the archive, an impasse can become a passage, in which limits are not confined to their materiality.

There's a name for all the people like me. They call us, the children whose parents went into exile, the post dictatorship generation. But that name implies the dictatorship is over. Even still, it's how I'd like to think of this story—this relation, alongside all the others—rather than consent to any literary category, any generic construction assumed by the organization of a text or the identity of its author. I'd like to remember to say that absence is the first condition of all representation. I'd like to remember to say that migration and exile propose an alternative to the institutionalization of the everyday and its policies of inclusion, integration, and validation, a decampment toward the *unspecified present.*

"Botched execution" as consequence and method: to botch is also to put together in a makeshift way. Botches linger, they intensify, become inflamed. In this mode of composition—discontinuous, accumulating, contrapuntal, momentary but also modular—I produce mistakes. When I work through botching, the text seems to dictate words to me, as if I were the secretary tasked with noting the coincidental residue—to express the wish while at the same time producing the wish—authorship as transcription. I want to say something about the displacement of desire here and the form or figure produced by our blur of movement, but what?

I write until I no longer have a face, only a tongue from which to speak. It is when I've redacted all but what is necessary that I can begin to tell my story. To tell it again. After so many years and so many tellings it feels impossible to know—impossible to say—what was heard or spoken or unspoken, when what would have been uttered was uttered as a moan.

Remember when the sun capsized and ... all I was left with was my notebook, which I could no longer see, even as I held it against my wrist where I sat, folding my right leg over my left knee, and thought about the mystery that would become this text.

I write words by clicking, photographing sensations as I alight upon them in my viewfinder.

On this app, users are allowed to revive the experience of using a disposable camera, heightening the anticipation of exposure by delaying it. Photos taken are not available to be seen until nine o'clock the next morning.

Reading *at a distance* articulates a suspended temporality between letters sent and received, read and returned. In the margins here, I've written: How can I articulate exile within correspondence?

The app's vast popularity suggests that what users really want is not instantaneity but the liminal zone of non-event, non-encounter. What users want is not momentary returns but the momentous occasion of what it means to be in a state of absence or longing: the return of loitering.

What is the difference between passage and threshold, threshold and corridor? The book as a meeting place for generational drift.

Years ago, the story about a Vietnamese farmer, wanting to hide from the rain, who found a hole and crawled in, only to find that the hole was endless. He kept crawling. What do I want to say about it? Nothing, except for a certain pleasure in passing. Wanting to alight upon the memory of receiving it, wanting to reprint the sound and cadence of its reception, to redistribute it, to turn this peculiar image into a set of words, to make it more familiar or more unfamiliar, to organize it across a strip of paper. To share that story with you.

Someone (my imagined reader) asks, That's all?
And I reply, That's everything.

Another writerly method: to draw attention to what I am not saying.

(Annotation as subject and method. Apotheosis of the text: when I can no longer distinguish my notes from the narrative. When the past is confused with its mediation. And I know it is done if it is incomplete.)

What is the difference between opposition and resemblance? In a mirror I see all that I am, which is everything I'm not. (What lasts is the convergence of inner and outer realities.)

my most disgraceful trait: an inability
to ever lose sight of myself

(Notion of the self-regarding text.)

In another version of this story, all the memories of my parents' childhoods, of their unreturnable homes, are in a few dozen rolls of film, which I never thought to develop until now.

If I showed you a page from my notebook you'd say, "Sometimes you'd think he'd never used a camera before."

This evening, I play a game and invite my students. The game is called *What I'm reading*. And I want them to guess. But I also want them to make me guess. I want them to collect image and sound and sign. To begin to think of themselves as collectors, but also as recorders: tasked with the pledge to play it back.

A trio of elements brought together by destiny and sealed by fate.

If we were still playing, I would offer you three options.

- ❑ a fantasy novel published in the 1980s
- ❑ the back of a jar of salsa
- ❑ a pamphlet for a New York City congressional campaign

A collector is someone who works in curation and juxtaposition. In this way, the making of a book, and writing in general, is a relief from having to be original.

like language, mother
(with a small M)
retains her secrets & it is
through her son
that she travels & continues
to live on

Translation as relationship, not equivalence (or equation) … [translation as] a mutually transformative process built upon displacement, not denial: a radical reinvention of the source as the trace.

How to give someone a memory of something they have never seen? Take a photo; destroy the source or model. Then the composition becomes memory and memorial.

I want to tell you the story of my childhood, and I'll leave a space here, on the opposite page, for you to tell me yours, and maybe we can allow ourselves this space, this time, to read together and to read the space itself, too, the time between our messages, as a necessary duration.

(The imaginary arrival when past interweaves with its persistent re-memberings, as if the child could return to the moment prior to actual flight, as if the child could return to the bodies belonging to the people they had come from.)

Remember J, who said or used to say poetry is not prose because of its formal properties, or because of its content and ambiguity, but because it allows musical elements (time, sound) to be introduced into the world of words.

How to exceed the limits of the visible and the audible within the arts of the skin and the flesh? Another way of asking this is asking what possibilities exist to make a text in which the power of hearing is spoken. In which the text does not speak but listens. I was after another possible writing, which is to say another possibility for feeling. Remember M, who told me it is because my cinema scarcely exists as cinema that I can make these films.

(Is it really acting, are they really actors if/when/since the roles they are supposed to play never exist prior to their performances, and the persons never quite know what they are fabricating at the moment of fabrication?)

Cut to an electronic advertisement (on the strip, in evening):

AUTOBIOGRAPHY AS THE BIG ~~REVEAL~~ RE-VEIL

I want to return to our discussion of imagination and chance, chance and the repercussions of the world as it is being remade.

Who was it who was it who told me words can give us back the earth which the earth had taken from us.

(As if the soundtrack were doubled, so that we could hear in the single expression [just quoted] still other meanings.)

As when color slips from image, when image slips from form.

each small & hallowed
task of the body
the smell of
damp grass, sourdough, butter left
sweating on a counter

& the air after
rain as cadence
from a window, ascendant
function of the sky
where I can openly

admit my desires
as if the landscape
of cloud & polluted
blue offers
a generous

crowd, one hundred or more
nights & their single
hypothesis: if I
am only readable that is recognizable that is
worthy to exist

in the weeks measured &
meted out to each community
of others like & unlike
me. neither
question nor antecedent clause

but rather conditional
statement that repeats once
a year. I mean in every
pledge of allegiance is
the confirmation of violence

what I ask of this text is what I ask
of all experience rendered in words
a moment however brief
of intensity, to be as coincident
as a daydream on the street corner

of our mid-afternoon, the reassuring
proximity of the present
& your hand here, turning
inward, asking
to be pliable like

lotion or the fold
of skin itself (want
to melt over you, under
you, I would bend to take you
in) you would ask about

the rhythm of
my pressure, indexing
our web by the like
-lihood & potency
of a leak, as if

the juxtaposition of foam
& my tendency to
equate prayer
with currency
could be held to account

let me try once more

there is never a poem. still less is there
a poem about something. there is only
a desire to be always both
writing & written, to be in the grip
of composition

you have to push harder

"he stuck the landing"

the unremembered attachment

scent or its after
taste   re

embedded parallel
to the current
camouflaged by shrubs
trees & power
lines our morning

pattern how we
listened as we strolled
for the drone
of the ocean
in truth

our proximity
to the garden
state parkway
& all its steady & unseeable
flow as when

a verb conjures without
subject or tense

we discover things
as a result of
their passing

imminence of the just
tempered by the injury
of postdated inscription

in the ordered
sequence of
a history / my negative

time
of flight
mode a hesitation

to call it
what it is
hardly ever hungry until

my sense of smell
kicks in
snuffing out

the narcotic
of narrative rhetoric &
its careful enunciation

of a singular I

like my least
conductive locker room
mementos

humiliation of the figurative
the hum
drum literal

those revving engines'

responsibility to transfer
the load "without
a hitch"

body behind
a screen &

the distasteful task
of asking

he was "saving himself"
for marriage

not the thing pictured
but the noetic tissue

which will rime
the image &

ready its
perception

on the outside

alterations of the breath
if a throat
awakens

the condescending lesson
of having always

to be hard
& a man

she said sorbet
may derive
from a latin verb
meaning to

suck up

lips whistling from afar
too much of a good thing

too much of my god
thing repetition

tending to difference
the way a hose
shepherds the drained

flesh how I lean
to heed
the motorized swells

& wavelets
swarm / veer / convey
I also like

young & uncertain
adjusting to desires
of his peers
the deictic surge

of your slackened blouse (blousy frock) (baggy fatigues)
fondling
memory into chance
appearance / drag

your favorite answer into the icon
box above & linger

predisposed
to say the silent
syllables of words
in public

I created the parts
of myself to glut
the whole that wasn't
whole—what would the world

become if I had only ever
accepted what I was
& will "forever"
be

    listless & overdue
for play we cool

the perishables
then lay

them out
according to

ascending density
remember to look up

dromomanic
metaleptic
biddable

I grow as you
approach / so don't
stop

& the unspoken call
there's no one in here & that

you have to push harder

my only insistence
the occasion

to render our terms
of legibility again

it was as if
we'd escaped our old lives

but recovered each other
in the new

(the trees there were
high & so closer
to heaven)

Acknowledgments

Windows 85 came together very quickly; *Rolling Windows* was an experience (experiment?) of duration. I'm grateful to many people for their support, guidance, and inspiration throughout the last decade, dating to at least June 2018, which is when this book begins, if it's true books ever really begin with writing or end in publication. I'd like to thank early readers of *Rolling Windows* for your care, insight, and generosity: Marwa Helal, Anthony Cody, and Jose-Luis Moctezuma. Ongoing conversations with Lilly Wu, Christodoulos Makris, Ry Cook, Rockwell Harwood, Reuben Gelley Newman, Tiffany Troy, Tai Nakamura, Miciah Hussey, A. Shaikh, Stù Watson, Roberto Harrison, Wayne Koestenbaum, Jay Gao, and Joseph Byrd continue to nourish these poems. Thanks, again, to Tiffany Troy, who translated "maybe she's born with it" into Chinese and performed the poem in Mandarin for the annual Queens Poetry Symposium, which convened at the Queens Public Library in Flushing on November 20, 2025.

The image of a security camera mounted on a building with palm trees swaying against reflecting panels that graces this book's cover was photographed by Nathan Dumlao. The epigraph by Édouard Glissant comes from his 1997 collection, *Traité du tout-monde*, which was translated into English by Celia Britton and published by Liverpool University Press as *Treatise on the Whole-World* in 2020. The interior image of the city street as seen against a supply store window was photographed by Rockwell Harwood. The illustrations used throughout "picture the arrière-garde" are in the public domain, sourced from Google Patents. See Jack Kadymir and Richard Schweitzer's lapsed patent for "Disposable underarm perspiration pad" (2002).

Thank you to the editors and readers of the following journals and exhibitions, where the sequences collected in this book, sometimes in different versions, first appeared:

"barbarian," *Michigan Quarterly Review* (MQR Mixtape) 14 (2024)

Parts of "rolling windows," *Poetry Project Newsletter* #283 (Winter 2026)

"the juxtaposition of foam," *The American Wing*, in collaboration with Postcollapse.art (2026)

"picture the arrière-garde" and "hypothesis of the leather jacket," *Denver Quarterly* 58.2 (2024)

"unexpectedly human" and "l'eclisse," *Explorations in Media Ecology* 25.1 (2026)

Parts of "and the laws that make us illegal," "picture the arrière-garde," and "the juxtaposition of foam," *Revel 1* (Winter 2024)

Parts of "restored late renaissance oil," "unexpectedly human," "and the laws that make us illegal," and "the juxtaposition of foam," *Revel 2* (Summer 2024)

ROOF BOOKS

the best in language since 1976

Recent & Selected Titles

- FALSE SPRING by Amie Zimmerman, 94 pp. $20
- CHATTY FOSSILS by Bob Perelman, 96 pp. $20
- IN THE REALM OF MOTES by Baptiste Gaillard, translated by Aditi Machado, 174 pp. $20
- WHAT TO CARRY INTO THE FUTURE by Susan Landers, 106 pp. $20
- ANYTHING WITH SPIRIT by isaiah a. hines, 104 pp. $20
- TUNES & TENS by Kit Robinson, 130 pp. $20
- THE FLOW OF THE POEM'S DISPLAY OF ITSELF by Carrie Hunter, 150 pp. $20
- WINDOWS 85 by Chris Campanioni, 160 pp. $20
- BUMBLEBEES by Deborah Meadows, 100 pp. $20
- THROUGH A WINDOW by Norman Fischer, 104 pp. $20
- SECRET SOUNDS OF PONDS by David Rothenberg, 138 pp. $29.95
- HAND ME THE LIMITS by Ted Rees, 130 pp. $20
- TGIRL.JPG by Sol Cabrini, 138 pp. $29.95
- THE POLITICS OF HOPE (After the War): Selected and New Poems by Dubravka Djuric, Biljana D. Obradovic (translator), 248 pp. $25
- BAINBRIDGE ISLAND NOTEBOOK by Uche Nduka, 148 pp. $20
- MAMMAL by Richard Loranger, 128 pp. $20
- EXCURSIVE by Elizabeth Robinson, 140 pp. $20
- I, BOOMBOX by Robert Glück, 194 pp. $20
- FOR TRAPPED THINGS by Brian Kim Stefans, 138 pp. $20
- TRUE ACCOUNT OF TALKING TO THE 7 IN SUNNYSIDE by Paolo Javier, 192 pp. $20
- THE NIGHT BEFORE THE DAY ON WHICH by Jean Day, 118 pp. $20
- MINE ECLOGUE by Jacob Kahn, 104 pp. $20
- SCISSORWORK by Uche Nduka, 150 pp. $20
- THIEF OF HEARTS by Maxwell Owen Clark, 116 pp. $20
- DOG DAY ECONOMY by Ted Rees, 138 pp. $20

Roof Books are published by Segue Foundation
For a complete listing of Roof Books, go to: roofbbooks.com
Roof Books are distributed by
Independent Publishers Group/IPGbook.com